Publication sponsored by
TSB Group plc

Glynn Williams

Hughes, Glyn

series

Publisher

MODERN
BRITISH
MASTERS

BERNARD JACOBSON GALLERY

On Poetry and Stone

I want to describe the sculpture of Glynn Williams as poetic, but find myself burdened with scruples over the use of such a word, as I do whenever it is applied as a metaphor.

Poets take pride in their medium which is the origin of an accolade that should be used more rarely than it is. Yet they approach the work and achievement of sculptors with, on the one hand awe, and on the other hand, envy. It is the substantiality of it. At bottom this was the reason why Rilke, one of the most spiritual and least rooted of poets, was so fascinated by Rodin, that he haunted his studio, worked as unpaid secretary, and wrote a book about the sculptor.

Poet and sculptor meet in the communality of art, where only artists can communicate. Their practices could not be further apart. The poet requires little in the way of materials, and may manage without them altogether. Plucked out of air, or spirit, and essentially oral, poetry has been composed on forced marches, as Mandelstam composed, or on chosen ones, as Wordsworth created The Prelude on his long walks. Poems are typically a finer distraction for the mind while supposedly occupied with other things, even if those 'other things' are the sheer necessity of staying alive. Presumably this is how Wilfred Owen composed in the First World War trenches. The words are all that matter; the way they are written down is irrelevant. Yet this art form has given us the metaphor, 'poetic'.

I introduce these ideas, in the first place not so much in order to generalise about poetry, but by its contrast to say something about sculpture, which is inherently non-conceptual. Sculpture is a working-out with an actual, physical material. At one period of his life, Glynn Williams, under the necessity of making long journeys by rail, tried to fill the time by making drawings for sculpture to be executed later, and ended by blaming the practice for taking his art up a blind alley. Beginning in the same crucible of the spirit as the poet's work, the sculptor's creation cannot merely be plucked out of the head and applied. A journeyman might indeed rough out the stone, but the carving must be done by the sculptor. He cannot 'dictate' the work, as an author might. Glynn Williams, in particular, has kept his faith in working with stone. His work, that is to say, aims right at the centre of what sculpture is.

Much of the time, a poet may feel anxious about not having something obvious and tangible with which to occupy himself. I do not mean that the devotion to the muse should not be total. On the contrary, that is the source of the anxiety. The preoccupation with poetry consumes the whole of life, but most of the time there is nothing to show for it. He tries other jobs, but finds himself on a dangerous tightrope, because he is unlikely to find one that can tolerate the necessary, constant distraction and half-distraction by the muse. Maybe he puts his poetry into another mould and writes novels, a form satisfyingly closer to sculpture because novel writing, too, absorbs time, work, and the novelist can probably show the visible evidence of materials, a workplace, a desk, a filing cabinet.

He is therefore teased by the existence of the man whose necessity is to spend immensely long hours with lumps of stone under his hands. The most resounding lesson that Rodin taught Rilke was "Il faut toujours travailler".

The fact that one can express oneself through it, through the work in itself, that one has something to "show", hour by hour, is enviable. Yet the amount of labour required of a sculptor in order to achieve anything, and the conditions under which he must do it, are awesome. So awesome, that the physicality of the work enters into the very nature of the art – and when that labour is carried off gracefully, it becomes one of the definitive joys received from sculpture.

That springing grace, when the airy spirit of the muse lifts this most gravitationally bound medium of them all, the medium that comes directly from the earth, is one of the specific delights of Glynn Williams's carving: that inventive spirit that can cut stone, as in the 1985 *Stone Rise East,* to a height of over six feet expressing an original and simply perceived idea, that of the boy balanced upside down on his own shoulders, and carry-off such inventions or perceptions time and time again. There is the mother and child enjoying a tug-of-war together in *Laughing, Pulling* of 1984; and the lovers lying, not conventionally on top of one another but stretched horizontally end to end, in the *Long Stone Couple* of 1988; and the bronze *Dreaming Woman* of 1991, to give further random examples.

It is that particular enshrinement of a spirit within the material – one that cannot be achieved without great gifts for the nature and craft of stone-carving – that I would describe as poetic. One recognises the presence of the muse, transcendent and earthy at one and the same time. The combination has much to do with what makes Glynn Williams's work, for me, for most people, indefinably but instantly loved. On March 15th, this year, Glynn Williams and I took a Sunday afternoon walk together through Greenwich Park. I asked him about the stone he uses almost exclusively: the limestone quarried in Lincolnshire and Rutland, at Ancaster and Clipsham – a district I know well from having lived in and built up an affection for it over several years. Already, I knew something about these quarries. They are part of the vein of limestone that became both necessary to, and in its nature an inspiration for, some of the great English cathedrals, from Lincoln to Salisbury, and for other buildings.

The quarries – nondescript, largely played-out, unregarded as they are today – were already hallowed ground to me. But when Glynn Williams, touched to his passion, began to talk, continuing for fifteen minutes on how the vein of limestone traverses England from north-east to south-west, yellow in Rutland and Lincolnshire, tinted slightly orange in the Cotswolds, disappearing under the Channel, surfacing in France where it is the stone out of which the great French cathedrals were built and carved, I found a new perspective opening to me. He spoke of the "fluidity" of the stone, making possible what could not be achieved in granite or marble: that distinctive quality of medieval art, the flowing marriage of building and sculpture. He talked also of one special quality of his favourite stone: that although it is soft enough to be easily cut, it can also acquire a hard polish, if required.

Glynn Williams's devotion to carving stone is total. He himself is partly bemused by his own gift. How easily a sculptor's life can be falsely romanticised! One patron thought it would be rather wonderful to watch him at work. "You wouldn't be able to stand it for ten minutes. The noise, the air clouded with stone dust," the sculptor replied. It is an unhealthy occupation. And then, there's the social danger of an obsession. To achieve anything, a sculptor has to work longer hours, more arduously, than other artists. He has little else to talk about, other than sculpture. Williams has not taken a holiday for years; what breaks he's had, have been to visit a gallery or a quarry. He remarked of Michelangelo's letters that they are full of excuses for not keeping engagements, because he had things to do in his studio.

Michelangelo, or any other sculptor from Phidias to Moore, would have felt totally at home with Williams's panegyric to Anglo-French limestone; probably it would have been the only contemporary conversation that would not have baffled them, when so much else has changed!

So much has changed, in fact, that probably Williams's fidelity to the traditional sculptor's material, stone, is the one subject that many of his contemporary sculptors *wouldn't* sympathise with, they being more at home with discussions about steel or fibre-glass, and regarding Williams's love as backward-looking.

It has to be recorded, for future generations to be puzzled by it, that Glynn Williams, as gifted and masterly a sculptor as you will find anywhere today, now in his maturity and with a large body of achievement to his credit, is often regarded as an embarrassment to the contemporary sculptural establishment. "Embarrassing" was the word used by Norman Rosenthal to describe Williams's position, when he was interviewed by Peter Jenkins for Modern Painters (Vol. 4, No. 2, Summer 1991). Waldemar Januszczak descended to insult when he attempted to define, also in Modern Painters, (Summer 1988 edition) Williams's work as, "A flight from the modern world into some dreadful arcadian stone-carver's rest-home": a description that is witty, seemingly truthful, and typical of the scoring against Williams that is carried on in the artistic press, but so clearly wide of the mark when one confronts the carvings with sensibilities open.

If Williams had continued in later life the carving of his youth, when his remarkable gifts were being tutored by his mentor Tom Wright in Wolverhampton in the late fifties, Januszczak's dismissal might have been accurate. Peter Fuller, also writing in Modern Painters, described Williams as, "born a virtuoso carver, one of those rare individuals who can cut, chisel, and find convincing sculptural forms with such facility that he is barely aware that he is gifted." The temptation to be merely a virtuoso carver must have been great. There was no-one else around who could exhibit the traditional skills, not merely so well, but so effortlessly, and so without self-regard.

It must have been his fine, basic sensibility and intelligence that urged him on beyond "mere" carver's ability and the confines of craftsmanship; that made him more than a second Tom Wright.

One of the myths about sculptors is that they are often phlegmatic workmen, illiterate, ill-educated, dyslexic perhaps, possessed only by a divine gift for the particular materials of their art. This is despite the examples of Michelangelo, who wrote great poetry, and of many other sculptors. Possibly because Glynn Williams is built like an ox, and has a way of puncturing pretensions with blunt talk and earthy humour, it is necessary to point out how broadly and how well educated he is. For example, in discussing James Joyce, I remarked that I had hardly met anyone other than Joyce scholars who have read Finnegan's Wake. "I have," answered Williams.

To such a sculptor as Sir Anthony Caro, for example, there is absolutely no point at all, and nothing intelligent, during the nineteen nineties, in carving human or animal figures, in traditional materials.

The least that can be said in answer is that more than one point of view might be legitimate – especially in the twentieth century, which has thrived upon eclecticism. But one certain claim must be made for Williams's work. He does not belong in any way to that cultural ghetto to which many would assign him. That is the ghetto of the naïve, or faux naïve, artist who is only part-conscious of what he is doing and blunders along unconscious of art's destiny. His response to contemporary sculptural mores is neither ignorant nor backward-looking nor negative. It is entirely positive, and forward-looking.

Perhaps it belongs more to the twenty-first century which, if history is anything to go by, is certain to be full of shocks and surprises for our present fin-de-siècle fashionables.

When Williams took up his sculpture professorship at the Royal College of Art, the accusation was made in some quarters that it would set sculpture back one hundred years. On the contrary, it is likely that Williams will turn out to be one of the few to preserve and advance certain sensibilities, intelligences and skills for the benefit of a future period.

Maybe with a sense of his own destiny in mind, Williams himself is fascinated by the shock that must have been felt at the dawn of the Renaissance when, after the long reign of a certain kind of rigid iconography, ancient sculpture was rediscovered and it was realised that there was no-one presently alive able to carve the kind of sculpture that had been left in abundance by a previous time.

Another of Williams's fascinations is with the centuries it took Greek sculpture, taking off from the massive stasis of Egyptian carving, to advance a single foot in front of the body, then to bend the body, and finally to achieve movement. In the light of this, Williams's versatility in showing the human body, or bodies in relationship to one another, in sculpturally surprising and illuminating ways, becomes especially interesting. Ways that are new to sculpture, and yet belong to a tradition. In our day, Williams's work is becoming increasingly valued because it evidently fulfils a requirement that few other sculptors are capable of satisfying. From a future point of view, it might seem that Williams's work is the growing point; or at least an inheritance that will shorten the struggle to rediscover what is in danger of being forgotten.

It is a truism that what is most revolutionary, most relevant and also most disturbing to the present day, – to any present day – is often not the latest novelty in art pulled out of the heads of ambitious strivers, but something that restores, reinterprets, revivifies, and reawakens a tradition. That is the reason why Henry Moore's youthful browsing in the British Museum proved so fruitful. The re-embodied principles of Egyptian and Mexican sculpture appeared as shocking innovations to Moore's contemporaries – especially, ironically, to the very people who regarded themselves as "traditionalists". Such rediscoveries are apparently the more shocking because they are at once simple, obvious, yet profound. The same might be said of Picasso. It took a later generation to accuse Moore of being too traditional, Picasso of being a plagiarist who ransacked the imagery of ancient art. A bitter irony!

I would argue that Glynn Williams's work restores the truest and strongest qualities of archaic sculpture.

When Glynn Williams grew out of his early experience of naturalism, when the young man inevitably ran into a dead-end there, it was to enter what he himself has acknowledged as "a dark night of the soul" – making abstract sculptures, not in natural and traditional materials, but in synthetics at one remove from nature, and already transformed. "Noxious fibreglass", as Peter Fuller put it. Though even many of these were sensual and erotic, true to Williams. One abstract sculpture, for instance, using obviously female forms, contained sponges loaded with cheap scent.

However, and in Williams's own words, the 1960s were a period when "I took the ten years of my earlier stone carved sculpture on a long detour into a nightmare of fibreglass stage sets showing off 'art ideas'". He developed a "conceptual" way of working – the ideas arising mentally and preconceived, rather than being discovered and growing out of a relationship with the nature of a particular block of stone. (Whimsically, he says that he blames this partly on having to teach in colleges scattered around Britain. Spending so much time on trains, therefore unable to carve, he used the time in making drawings for sculptures to be completed later.)

Williams was working for a time in what is today as conventional a mode as were the innumerable, writhing, quasi-Laocoons in bronze or stone to European sculpture at the last end-of-the century.

Williams has argued cogently that we are at present living in a parallel, decadent period. Much of his argument is laid out in the text of his Inaugural Lecture as Professor of Sculpture at the Royal College of Art in 1991, (published under the title, 'On Kicking Out the Cuckoo', by the Bernard Jacobson Gallery). The substance of the parallel that Williams draws is that, as at the end of the nineteenth century when nature was copied or repeated in art, naturalistically but virtually without comment other than perhaps a sentimental gloss, so today contemporaneous, synthetic materials are exhibited without comment, simply as themselves, in order to speak for themselves. This, Williams feels, is a hallmark of decadence, today as it was at the end of the nineteenth century. At best, such art might be a comment on art – he cites as an example Duchamp exhibiting a urinal – but, timely or interesting as that may or may not be, it is not in itself art. The element that is missing is that of transformation.

With later wisdom, Williams looks back at this period of his work with the claim that "*all* the stages of a journey are necessary."

Perhaps the one harm this diversion into conventional sculptural modes did for him was to cause him to be picked upon as a renegade from Conceptualism by his erstwhile confederates when he changed his mind. Deserting Conceptualism, he was championed by Peter Fuller – probably as earnestly and enthusiastically for his desertion, as others have heavily criticised him for it. It is this position that has brought him under savage attack for his present day lyrical realism, whereas other less gifted, less versatile, naturalistic sculptors have been praised and left in peace from the often arbitrary and irrelevant attacks launched against Williams – whose position, in this respect, is anomalous to that of David Bomberg who, when he turned to landscape painting as his reaction to the machine-made horror of the First World War, was criticised as an apostate from the modern movement, baffling because originally he had been the most promising and intelligent of its younger exponents before the War. It took a later generation than Bomberg's to see that his apparent reaction was in fact the growing point of British art.

So, I believe, it might come to seem with Williams. But, as he himself sees so clearly, it was that passage through the Slough of Conceptualism that created the gap in his past, after which he could think again about what his sculpture should be. A common criticism of Williams, that he is another Epstein or Gaudier-Brzeska, might be true of his apprentice pieces, but certainly not of what he has produced since 1978.

That was the date on which Williams set eyes upon the Etruscan *Man On A Sea Horse* in Rome. In this, a small figure rides the front part of a piece of colossal, muscular curve of stone, which has far more presence and force than the figure.

There were two leads for Williams in this sculpture.

Following the first one, he attempted to echo, in abstract terms, the power of that curve of stone. In his act of homage, he fell into a puzzling quagmire consequent upon abstraction. An abstraction could be taken in too many ways; it was "awash with ambiguities".

Williams found that he had passed through a "one-way door"; he had deserted his sculptural confrères and was back with unambiguous, figurative expression

Well, not back. There was a new ambition on the horizon – to create figurative sculpture that avoided what he calls "the nostalgia of naturalism".

There was another lesson in the *Man On A Sea Horse*. The little figure gained its potency, its powerful sense of looking forward, thus carrying the movement of the sculpture onwards – because of the accident that the sculpture was broken. The sea horse's head, that would have towered over and blocked the figure's gaze, stopping it from moving on and thus, conceivably, hampering the rhythm of the sculpture, was missing.

This had happened by accident, but the lesson for Williams was that a sculptural form is not always preconceived. In other words, he had moved from naturalistic representation, imitating appearances, to a kind of realism. By which I mean, to interpreting essences of reality, and creating not an imitation of a subject, but an alternative matching reality which we may call "sculpture".

From this point began the versatility of Williams's mature work, one of the most characteristic features of which is his manner of breaking or opening the sculpture in various ways; of cutting a piece of sculpture up, and reassembling it.

One of his reasons for doing this goes right back to that first revelation of the *Man On A Sea Horse*. It is to concentrate the essence – as in the 1988 *Pieta,* now in the crypt of Worcester Cathedral. It is a principle of all art forms, that what does not add to the work, dilutes it. The *Pieta* began as a larger work, with a large vertical mother holding the sagging, horizontal figure. The figure was boldly, simply sawn through, and the maternal form discarded, to give it the intensity possessed by the final work.

Much of this hacking and sawing has been the product of an art-historical exercise, and it is here that Williams's knowledge of all art has come to his aid. Moore made sculptured versions of the small Cézanne *Bathers* which he said was one of his most loved possessions, so this must be claimed as an antecedent to Williams's variations on famous paintings, but which other sculptor has done it so productively? In 1986, there came his version of Velázquez' 'Rokeby' *Venus*. There have been sculptured interpretations of Matisse and Courbet. And, it seems, endlessly productively, he carved the version of Picasso's *Demoiselles d'Avignon* of 1989.

Williams's sawn and simplified carving of this has proved to be a second of those "one-way doors" through which he passed after *Man On A Sea Horse*. At first sight, his *Two Girls From 1907* (after *Les Demoiselles d'Avignon*) appears to be an intelligent and interesting comment upon Cubism.

More importantly, what it has led to is a great leap forward in Williams's endeavour to let light into sculpted form. It is this, as much as anything else, that marks out Williams's later work, or indeed any really good sculpture. It is concerned with mass, but it does not consist of masses lumped, in dead fashion, over a stone core – that, in a phrase, is what typifies all bad sculpture. As a technique for letting light into sculpture, and for creating a sense of lightness, of mass combined with weightlessness, of flow, his technique of sawing, splitting, joining up in unnaturalistic ways, is superb.

Also, these disjointed stones, forms sliding against one another, are an original way of creating movement. The whole process is far more than an art-historical exercise.

I have remarked on how, almost uniquely, Williams has allowed himself to be influenced by the art of painters.

Similarly remarkable is the frequency with which a Williams sculpture is horizontal, and to be viewed close to the floor.

Traditionally, sculpture is assumed to consist usually of masses rising vertically, because that is what most of the world's sculpture does, no matter what its scale. That is because it most traditionally has a monumental function. It exists to justify pomp and pride, and is to be looked up to in awe. Therefore, when Glynn Williams stretches a sculpture out horizontally, lays it close to the floor, or perhaps with just enough clearance to allow the light to pierce it, enough also to give it dignity, instead of gazing up in awe or even in fear, the spectator looks downwards, encouraged to feel affection and tenderness – as with the beautiful *Morning* of 1987, the two lovers awaking with their feet crossed in ecstasy or, at least, joy. As in the *Head And Arms* of 1988 – again, a carving of lovers; and the *Long Stone Couple* of the same year.

In the end, and combined with the sculptural expertise, adventurousness and joy, it is this tenderness – "the true voice of feeling" – that makes Glynn Williams's work at one with the best of archaic sculpture. What moves us in Minoan or Etruscan carving, stirs us in Glynn Williams's work, makes it wanted, and will make it still wanted, when much of the fashionable gesturing of our time has passed away.

GLYN HUGHES

Glyn Hughes's poems have been a Poetry Book Society Recommendation. His first novel, *Where I Used To Play On Green,* won the Guardian Fiction Prize and the David Higham Prize. *The Antique Collector* (1990/1991) was shortlisted for the Whitbread Novel of the Year and for the James Tait Black Prize. His most recent novel, *Roth*, explores the lives of a seventy-one year old painter and his painter wife, and is about the masculine and feminine in art. It was published by Simon & Schuster in June this year.

SCULPTURE

1

RASPBERRY QUEEN, 1960

pink velvet

72 x 50 x 30ins/182.8 x 127 x 76.2cms

PROVENANCE

The Welsh Arts Council

EXHIBITED

Glynn Williams, ICA Gallery, London, 1967
Welsh Arts Council Exhibition, Cardiff, 1967
Richard Demarco Gallery, Edinburgh, 1968
Glynn Williams Retrospective, Sculpture at Margam, South Wales, 1992

2

THE RED BALLOON, 1968

fibreglass, mirror plastic, cloth

84 x 168 x 72ins/213.3 x 426.7 x 182.8cms

EXHIBITED

Midland Group Gallery, Nottingham, 1968

3

RAFT, 1970

fibreglass

96 x 96 x 84ins/243.8 x 243.8 x 213.3cms

PROVENANCE

The Welsh Arts Council

EXHIBITED

Glynn Williams, Serpentine Gallery, London, 1972
Glynn Williams, Ferens Art Gallery, Hull, 1974
Glynn Williams, Park Square Gallery, Leeds, 1974
Glynn Williams, Sheffield Polytechnic Gallery, 1974
Wakefield Festival, 1977
Glynn Williams, Oriel Gallery, Cardiff, 1978
Glynn Williams Retrospective, Sculpture at Margam, South Wales, 1992

4

EARLY VICTORIA, 1976

Portland stone

56 x 36 x 30ins/142.2 x 91.4 x 76.2cms

EXHIBITED

Inaugural Exhibition, Yorkshire Sculpture Park, 1977
Glynn Williams. Oriel Gallery, Cardiff, 1978
Glynn Williams Retrospective, Sculpture at Margam, South Wales, 1992

5

SADDLE-BACK, 1976

constructed wood

48 x 48 x 62ins/121.9 x 121.9 x 157.4cms

EXHIBITED

Cannizaro Park Annual Sculpture Exhibition, Wimbledon, 1978

6

SEA RIDER, 1979

Ancaster weatherbed stone

60 x 60 x 30ins/152.4 x 152.4 x 76.2cms

PROVENANCE

Peterborough Development Corporation

EXHIBITED

Cannizaro Park Annual Sculpture Exhibition, Wimbledon, 1979
Contemporary Sculpture, Hounslow Civic Centre, 1981

7

HOLDING, RISING, PROTECTING, 1981

Ancaster stone

72 x 30 x 26ins/182.8 x 76.2 x 66cms

PROVENANCE

Collection Tom Bendhem

EXHIBITED

Attitudes, Yorkshire Sculpture Park, 1981
Cannizaro Park Annual Sculpture Exhibition, Wimbledon, 1982
Glynn Williams, Piccadilly Festival, London, 1985
Glynn Williams Retrospective, Sculpture at Margam, South Wales, 1992

8

HUNTER, 1981

Ancaster stone

60 x 48 x 24ins/152.4 x 121.9 x 60.9cms

PROVENANCE

Grisedale Theatre Trust, Cumbria

EXHIBITED

Attitudes, Yorkshire Sculpture Park, 1981
Cannizaro Park Annual Sculpture Exhibition, Wimbledon, 1983
Great Linfind Sculpture Walk, Milton Keynes, 1984
Glynn Williams, Piccadilly Festival, London, 1985
Glynn Williams Retrospective, Sculpture at Margam, South Wales, 1992

9

SQUATTING, HOLDING, LOOKING, 1982

Ancaster stone

48 x 36 x 30ins/121.9 x 91.4 x 76.2cms

PROVENANCE

Milton Keynes General Hospital

EXHIBITED

Attitudes, Yorkshire Sculpture Park, 1981
Glynn Williams, Piccadilly Festival, London, 1985
Glynn Williams Retrospective, Sculpture at Margam, South Wales, 1992

10

SHOUT, 1982

Ancaster stone

65 x 48 x 39ins/165.1 x 121.9 x 99cms

PROVENANCE

Sculpture at Margam

EXHIBITED

Glynn Williams, Blond Fine Art, London, 1982 (catalogue no.13)
Glynn Williams, Piccadilly Festival, London, 1985
Glynn Williams Retrospective, Sculpture at Margam, South Wales, 1992

11

HANDSTAND, 1982

Ancaster stone

24 x 7 x 8ins/60.9 x 17.7 x 20.3cms

PROVENANCE

Collection Tom Bendhem

EXHIBITED

Glynn Williams, Blond Fine Art, London, 1982 (catalogue no.9)

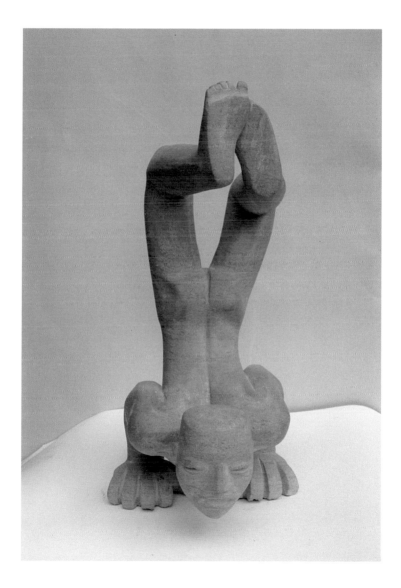

12

SISTERS, 1982

Clipsham stone

72 x 40 x 24ins/182.8 x 101.6 x 60.9cms

EXHIBITED

Glynn Williams, Blond Fine Art, London, 1982 (catalogue no.10)
Sculpture in a Country Park, Margam Park, 1983
Glynn Williams, Piccadilly Festivai, London, 1985
Feeling Through Form, Barbican Sculpture Court, London, 1986
Cutting Edge, Manchester City Art Gallery, 1989
Modern Masters, Bernard Jacobson Gallery, 1989
Glynn Williams Retrospective, Sculpture at Margam, South Wales, 1992

13

THREE HANDS, 1982

Ancaster Stone

36 x 14 x 14ins/91.4 x 35.5 x 35.5cms

EXHIBITED

Glynn Williams, Blond Fine Art, London, 1982 (catalogue no.12)
Contemporary Carving, Plymouth Art Centre, 1984 (touring)
Bluecoat Gallery, Liverpool, 1984
Glynn Williams, Piccadilly Festival, London, 1985
Feeling Through Form, Barbican Sculpture Court, London, 1986
Glynn Williams Retrospective, Sculpture at Margam, South Wales, 1992

14

SITTING STILL, 1983

Ancaster stone

40 x 36 x 24ins/101.6 x 91.4 x 60.9cms

PROVENANCE

Middlesbrough Council

EXHIBITED

Glynn Williams, Blond Fine Art, London, 1983
Figures in a Garden, Yorkshire Sculpture Park, 1984
Glynn Williams, Piccadilly Festival, London, 1985
Glynn Williams Retrospective, Sculpture at Margam, South Wales, 1992

15

STONE RISE EAST, 1985

Ancaster stone

72 x 60 x 36ins/182.8 x 152.4 x 91.4cms

EXHIBITED

Glynn Williams, Bernard Jacobson Gallery, London, 1985
Corner House Gallery, Manchester, 1985
Feeling Through Form, Barbican Sculpture Court, London, 1986
Cutting Edge, Manchester City Art Gallery, 1989
Summer Show, Royal Academy of Art, London, 1990
Glynn Williams, Northern Centre for Contemporary Art, Sunderland, 1991
Glynn Williams Retrospective, Sculpture at Margam, South Wales, 1992

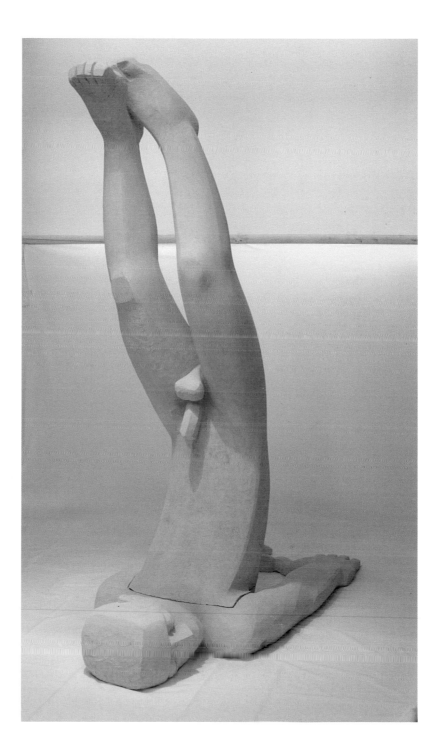

16

WOMAN WITH MIRROR (after Velázquez), 1986

Ancaster stone

56 x 19 x 18ins/142.2 x 48.2 x 45.7cms

PROVENANCE

Collection Roger and Cathy Wills

EXHIBITED

Glynn Williams, Bernard Jacobson Gallery, London, 1986
Glynn Williams, Artiste Gallery, Bath, 1987
Glynn Williams, Bernard Jacobson Gallery, London, 1989 (catalogue illus.)
Cutting Edge, Manchester City Art Gallery, 1989

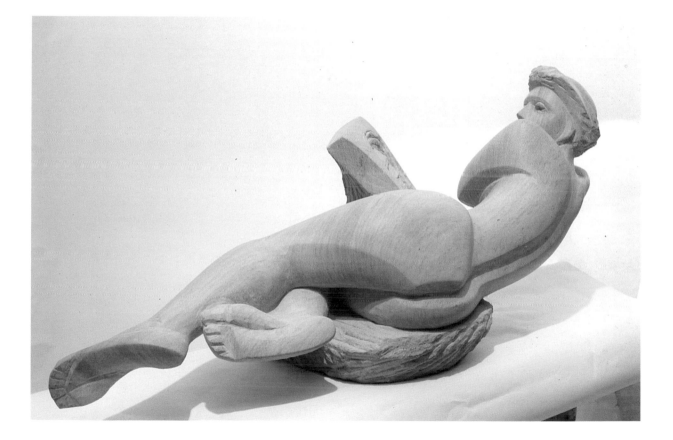

17

MORNING No.2, 1987/88

Ancaster weatherbed stone

88 x 47 x 15ins/223.5 x 119.3 x 38.1cms

18

STONE BRIDGE, 1988

Hoptonwood stone

70 x 21 x 17ins/177.8 x 53.3 x 43.1cms

PROVENANCE

Collection Pat and Michael York

EXHIBITED

Glynn Williams, Bernard Jacobson Gallery, London, 1989 (catalogue illus.)

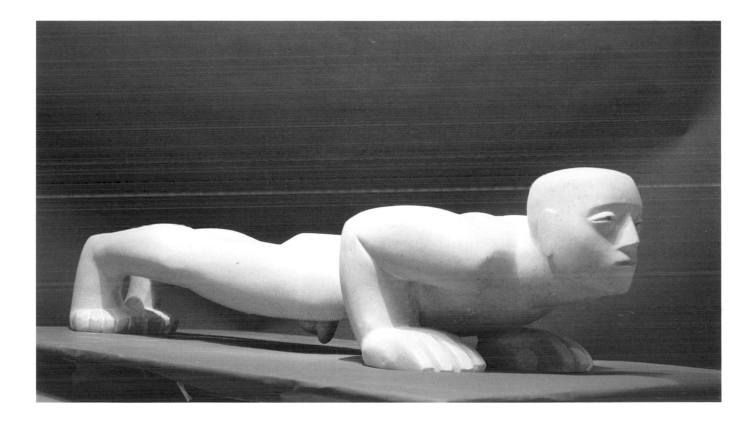

19

STONE BRIDGE No.2, 1988

Ancaster stone

19 x 10 x 6ins/48.2 x 25.4 x 15.2cms

PROVENANCE

Collection David and Janice Blackburn

EXHIBITED

Glynn Williams, Bernard Jacobson Gallery, London, 1989 (catalogue illus.)
Glynn Williams Retrospective, Sculpture at Margam, South Wales, 1992

20

HEADS AND ARMS, 1988

Hornton stone

17 x 11 x 13 ins/43.1 x 27.9 x 33cms

PROVENANCE

Private Collection, London

EXHIBITED

Glynn Williams, Bernard Jacobson Gallery, London, 1989 (catalogue illus.)

21

WOMAN WITH PLAIT, 1988

Hoptonwood stone

29 x 28 x 25ins/73.6 x 71.1 x 63.5cms

PROVENANCE

T.S.B. Group plc

EXHIBITED

Glynn Williams, Bernard Jacobson Gallery, London, 1989 (catalogue illus.)

22

SOPHIE SITTING, 1990

Hoptonwood stone

60 x 36 x 24ins/152.4 x 91.4 x 60.9cms

EXHIBITED

Sculpture at Salisbury Cathedral, Chichester Festival, 1991
Glynn Williams, Bernard Jacobson Gallery, London, 1991
Glynn Williams Retrospective, Sculpture at Margam, South Wales, 1992

23

OPENING CHESTNUT BUD, 1991

Portland stone

48 x 24 x 20ins/121.9 x 60.9 x 50.8cms

PROVENANCE

Estate of Peter Fuller (memorial carving)

24

PORTRAIT WITH FLOWERS, 1991

bronze

40 x 37 x 26ins/101.6 x 94 x 66cms

edition of 5

25

DREAMING WOMAN, 1991

bronze

28 x 10 x 16ins/71.1 x 25.4 x 40.6cms

edition of 5

EXHIBITED

Glynn Williams, Bernard Jacobson Gallery, London, 1991 (catalogue no.7)
Glynn Williams Retrospective, Sculpture at Margam, South Wales, 1992

26

PAPAGENO, 1991

Doulting stone

24 x 18 x 6ins/60.9 x 20.3 x 15.2cms

PROVENANCE

Collection David Bowie

EXHIBITED

Glynn Williams, Bernard Jacobson Gallery, London, 1991

27

MOTHER AND CHILD, 1991

bronze

11 x 9 x 10ins/27.9 x 22.8 x 25.4cms

edition of 7

EXHIBITED

Glynn Williams, Bernard Jacobson Gallery, London, 1991 (catalogue no.5)
Glynn Williams Retrospective, Sculpture at Margam, South Wales, 1992

28

WOMAN IN CHAIR, 1991

Doulting stone

42 x 38 x 20ins/106.6 x 96.5 x 50.8cms

EXHIBITED

Glynn Williams, Bernard Jacobson Gallery, London, 1991 (catalogue no.4)
Glynn Williams Retrospective, Sculpture at Margam, South Wales, 1992

29

ACROBATS, 1991

bronze

80 x 24 x 20ins/203.2 x 60.9 x 50.8cms

edition of 3

30

DAY DREAMER, 1991

bronze

17 x 6 x 7ins/43.1 x 15.2 x 17.7cms

edition of 5

EXHIBITED

Glynn Williams, Bernard Jacobson Gallery, London, 1991
Glynn Williams Retrospective, Sculpture at Margam, South Wales, 1992

31

SITTING, HOLDING, LOOKING, 1991

bronze

36 x 36 x 24ins/91.4 x 91.4 x 60.9cms

edition of 5

EXHIBITED

Glynn Williams, Bernard Jacobson Gallery, London, 1991 (catalogue no.8)
Glynn Williams Retrospective, Sculpture at Margam, South Wales, 1992

32

TWO GIRLS FROM 1907 (after Picasso) No.2, 1992

bronze

74 x 24 x 24ins/187.9 x 60.9 x 60.9cms

edition of 3

EXHIBITED

Glynn Williams Retrospective, Sculpture at Margam, South Wales, 1992

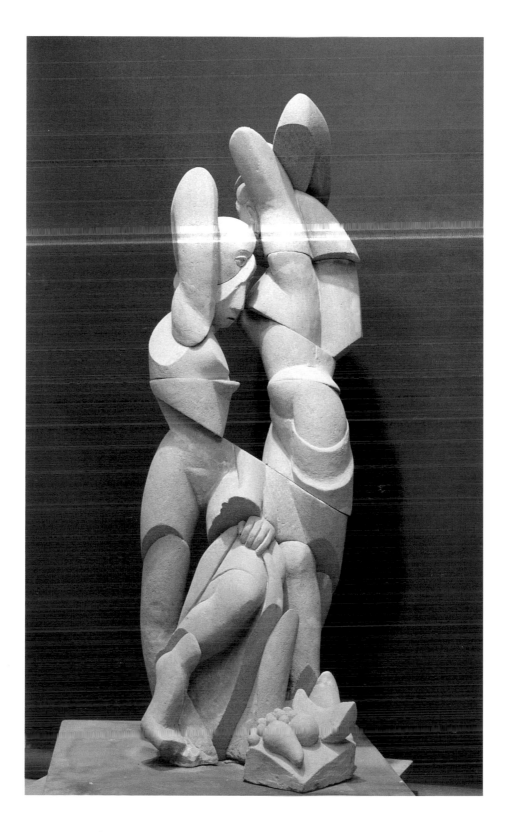

DRAWINGS

33

WOMAN WITH ARMS RAISED, 1989

charcoal on paper

40 x 27ins/101.6 x 68.5cms

34

LEANING HEAD, 1986

charcoal on paper

22 x 30ins/55.8 x 76.2cms

PROVENANCE

Private Collection

EXHIBITED

Glynn Williams, Bernard Jacobson Gallery, 1988

35

HEAD AND ARMS, 1988

charcoal on paper

22 x 30ins/55.8 x 76.2cms

36

SEATED WOMAN, 1990

charcoal on paper

40 x 27ins/101.6 x 68.5cms

SOME DATES FROM A PERSONAL BIOGRAPHY

1939   Born on 30 March in Shrewsbury and moved to
        Wolverhampton in June
        War was declared in September

1944   Started at a small church school in Penn village.
        First day a box full of slates was distributed to all us
        newcomers (there was no paper). I was early and got
        a new shiny black one. Latecomers had to have
        much used chalky grey ones. We were given white
        chalk to draw with on the slate. The teacher drew a
        horse on the large class blackboard and wrote
        DOBBIN under it and made us all copy it. When I
        finished my version it was taken from me by an
        excited teacher and rushed to the headmaster who
        kept it. I never saw it again and I had to get another
        slate from the box. Only the greyest of grey
        remained – my first lesson in what happens when
        you show off

1950   Passed the 11-plus and went to Wolverhampton
        Grammar School. Didn't excel at much except art
        and PE

1952   Mother died after a long fight with cancer

1954   Student came to the Grammar School to do his
        teacher training practice. Instead of Charlie Viner's
        demanding pencil studies we had a jazz record
        played to us, were given paints and large pieces of
        paper and asked to paint what the music meant (?)
        to us. This was my first encounter with the polarised
        opinions on what is or is not the right way to look at
        or make art

1956   Passed enough GCEs to get a place at
        Wolverhampton College of Art. Imagine doing art
        and nothing else all week – it was all I wanted in
        the world

        The first life class came and went without that
        frisson I had been led to expect. Pity really – life
        drawing at best is akin to a love affair and should be
        conducted in private with just the two participants.
        The human body is the centre of everything in art
        and most else

1958   I chose sculpture to specialise in for the next two
        years based entirely on my preference for the staff
        teaching in that department. I had never really done
        very much in three dimensions. Met Tom Wright,
        sculptor, who was teaching at the college part-time.
        He was an excellent sculptor who became a father
        figure to me

1960   Hitch-hiked to Spain – saw Gaudi's Cathedral in
        Barcelona and was knocked out by it – and still am.
        Visited Paris and the Musée Rodin – a lasting
        memory

Saw the Picasso Exhibition at the Tate Gallery –
breathtaking. Picasso always sends me back to the
studio to work

Exchanged a small stone carving for a large but
broken Ibo Elephant Mask – marvellous; my first
piece of African sculpture

1961   Awarded Rome Scholarship and went to Rome where
        I was given a studio in the British school. Made lots
        of sculpture and travelled around Italy

1962   Made a long round trip in small Fiat car with the
        artist Peter Freeth and an Australian architect
        through Turkey and Greece, Bulgaria, Yugoslavia, on
        to Venice and so back to Rome – marvellous

        Met Heather Woodhall who was in Rome on an
        Italian Government Scholarship – later on that year
        had a very romantic summer in the small hill
        village of Anticoli Corado just south of Tivoli

        Discovered the Etruscan Museum in the Villa Guillia
        in Rome and from then on visited it three or four
        times a week – it was and is my favourite museum
        in Rome

        Tom Wright died – made me cross as well as sad as
        there was so much that I wanted to discuss with him

1963   Returned to England and married Heather
        Began part-time teaching in various art colleges

1964   Victoria born. Moved to Leeds and began teaching
        at the art college; a very rich art community then
        with Norbert Lynton, Alan Davie, Terry Frost, Hubert
        Dalwood and later John Walker, Dennis Creffield and
        many more. Saw a copy of André Malraux's *Musée
        Imaginaire de la Sculpture Mondial* – what a
        wonderful sculpture handbook

1966   Sophie born

1969   Exhibited in a show at the ICA called *Young and
        Fantastic* and I designed an entrance installation
        for the show when it travelled to New York. Visited
        New York for the installation and sold a sculpture
        for the first time to a private collector – good place
        New York!

1970   Moved to London. Lived in Islington and rented a
        studio in Shoreditch with John Maine, Richard
        Rome, Derek Boshier, Lee Grandjean, Anish Kapoor
        and Martin Ward

1976   Appointed to run the Sculpture Department at
        Wimbledon School of Art. Started to build up a
        department of clear aims and attitudes towards
        sculpture, as opposed to the wash of pluralism that
        was beginning to flood most other art colleges

1977 Met Anthony Caro in a forum at St Martin's Sculpture Department – very impressed with his formal and analytical eye, also surprised by his openness and exploratory ability

Met Peter Fuller. I had read his controversial articles in *Art Monthly* and invited him to Wimbledon to take part in a seminar. We argued a lot that day and every day that we met after that until his untimely death. He became a most supportive, if provocative, friend

1981 *Attitudes* exhibition at Yorkshire Sculpture Park – I showed three new figures and in doing so felt very vulnerable. I had suddenly moved away from the group of sculptors to which I had associated and into a space of my own. Many people found my shift disquieting and my new works were received in very strange ways. Nick Serota, Director of the Whitechapel Art Gallery visited my studio and included two of my works in his *British Sculpture* exhibition; one piece from 1977 – an abstract wood construction, but more importantly a very new figure carving in stone. This little carving was the oddest thing in the show, sticking out like a sore thumb alongside Bill Woodrow, Tony Cragg and Anish Kapoor in the last room of the exhibition

1984 Invited by the British Council to represent Great Britain in the 3rd Kotara Takamura Grand Prize Exhibition in Japan. Visited Japan and made a television programme there. I enjoyed the country, the architecture and the food a great deal

1985 Met Bernard Jacobson who has been a great support and encouragement to me and is a good friend. Rekindled a lapsed friendship with Mike and Kate Westbrook whose music is such wonder, always joyous, even funny and with whom we have shared many happy meals and glasses of wine

1986 Epstein exhibition at the Whitechapel – *Lazarus* at the end of the upper gallery looked as good as I have ever seen it. What a good 'rough-arsed' carver he was

1987 Rodin exhibition at the Hayward Gallery; a master indeed – but a nineteenth-century master for the most part

David Smith exhibition at the Whitechapel; wonderful to see how subject matter was always there in the sculptures despite what the abstract art world says

Fernand Léger exhibition at the Whitechapel – what a marvellous sculptor he could have been if he had moved into 3-dimension properly

1990 On 28 April Peter Fuller was killed when the chauffeur driven car in which he was travelling left the road. Much has been said elsewhere in tribute to Peter's enormous effect upon the art world. I was convinced that he was to have been the 'herald' on the gateway into the new millenium. Now we will have to try and do it without him

Just as I'm contemplating leaving art education, having built up Wimbledon Sculpture to a strength as good as I can imagine, I accepted the appointment of Professor of Sculpture at the Royal College of Art. There's such a lot that needs doing I couldn't refuse. I must be mad!

1991 Completed *Opening Chestnut Bud*, now sitting on Peter Fuller's grave in the little church in Stowlangtoft , Suffolk. George Patterson conducted a short ceremony when the sculpture was unveiled. It was a lovely sunny day with a good crowd of friends. It was a year exactly since Peter died and all the chestnut trees in the village were in bloom

Began cutting up and reassembling stone carvings and making sculptures with a view to cutting them apart. Extending to myself a new licence with my subject matter

The exhibition at Bernard Jacobson Gallery of my new sculpture once more seemed to upset some of those who had become familiar with the previous carvings but also brought a whole lot of new appreciation. Work cannot stand still

Delivered my inaugural lecture as Professor of Sculpture at the Royal College of Art. I 'laid out my stall' for all to see in as clear a way as possible. I made an argued stand against the philosophic statement posing as sculpture. It was a 'full house' and certainly polarised opinions

1992 Made *Open Hands* the biggest sculpture I have ever made. It will stand either side of the pathway at Margam Park and act as a gateway entrance to my exhibition there

ONE-MAN EXHIBITIONS

1967   ICA Gallery, London
1972   Serpentine Gallery, London
1974   Ferens Art Gallery, Hull
       Sheffield Polytechnic Gallery
       Park Square Gallery, Leeds
1977   Wakefield Festival
1978   Oriel Gallery, Cardiff
1982   Blond Fine Art Gallery, London
1985   Piccadilly Festival, St. James' Church
       Gardens, London
       Bernard Jacobson Gallery, London
1986   Bernard Jacobson Gallery, London
1987   Artsite Gallery, Bath
1988   Bernard Jacobson Gallery, London
1991   Bernard Jacobson Gallery, London
       Northern Centre for Contemporary Art,
       Sunderland
1992   Sculpture at Margam, South Wales

SELECTED GROUP EXHIBITIONS

1962   Palazzo delle Esposizioni, Rome
1964   Welsh Arts Council Exhibition, Cardiff
       (Sculpture Prize)
1965   Welsh Arts Council Exhibition, Cardiff
1967   Welsh Arts Council Exhibition, Cardiff
       (Sculpture Prize)
1968   Midland Group Gallery, Nottingham
       Richard Demarco Gallery, Edinburgh
1969   Park Square Gallery, Leeds
       British Contemporary Art, ICA London,
       then touring New York and Toronto
       Play Orbit, ICA London
1970   *Towards Sculpture*, Welsh Arts Council
       Exhibition, Cardiff
1972   Scottish Arts Council Exhibition, Edinburgh
       and Glasgow
       Eleven Sculptors One Decade, touring
       Arts Council Exhibition
       International Print Biennale, Bradford
1973   *International Drawing Biennale*, Middlesbrough
1975   *Envelopes*, JPL Fine Art, London
       Bradford City Art Gallery

1976   Welsh Arts Council Exhibition, Cardiff
       Serpentine Gallery, London
1977   Yorkshire Sculpture Park Opening Exhibition
1978   *New Sculpture*, Ikon Gallery, Birmingham
1979   *Wood*, Yorkshire Sculpture Park
       Current British Sculpture, The Norwich School
       of Art Gallery, Norwich
1981   *British Sculpture in the 20th Century*,
       Whitechapel Art Gallery, London
       Contemporary Sculpture, Hounslow
       Civic Centre
       Attitudes, Yorkshire Sculpture Park
       Blond Fine Art Winter Exhibition, London
1983   *Sculpture in a Country Park*, Margam Park,
       South Wales
       Drawing in Air, Sunderland Arts Centre (touring)
       International Sculpture Symposium,
       Yorkshire Sculpture Park
       Leinster Fine Art Gallery, London
1984   Bluecoat Gallery, Liverpool
       Figures in a Garden, Yorkshire Sculpture Park
       British Council representative in the
       3rd Kotaro Takamura Grand Prize Exhibition,
       Japan
       Contemporary Carving, Plymouth Arts Centre
       (touring)
       Sculptors Drawing, Scottish Arts Council
       touring Exhibition
       Sculpture in a Cathedral, Canterbury Festival
       Blond Fine Art Summer Exhibition
1985   *British Artists in Italy*, touring exhibition
       Hands, Anne Berthoud Gallery, London
       Rocks and Flesh, touring exhibition of
       drawings, curated by Peter Fuller
       British Drawing, Bernard Jacobson Gallery,
       New York
       Visual Aid, 100 Artists for Ethiopia, Royal
       Academy, London
       Opening Exhibition, Cornerhouse Gallery,
       Manchester
1986   *Feeling through Form*, Barbican Sculpture
       Court (touring)
       Sculpture in a City, Artsite Gallery, Bath
       Contemporary Figurative Sculpture,
       Castlefields Gallery, Manchester
1987   *Self Portraits*, Artsite Gallery, Bath (touring)
       7th International Small Sculpture, Budapest

1988 *Mother and Child,* Lefevre Gallery, London
Stone Works, Powys Castle Grounds, Wales
Recent Acquisitions, Tate Gallery, London
Birthright, Artsite Gallery, Bath
Libesc 88, International Sculpture Exhibition,
Lisbon

1989 *Cutting Edge,* Manchester City Art Gallery
Roche Court Sculpture Garden, Wiltshire
Modern Masters, Bernard Jacobson Gallery,
London
Art Since the War, Ferens Art Gallery, Hull
Drawing the Line, Artists Against Apartheid,
Merz Gallery, London

1990 ICA Benefit Auction, Sotheby's, London
Tribute to Peter Fuller, Bernard Jacobson
Gallery, London
Royal Academy Summer Exhibition, London
Heads, Hands, Feet, Margam Park,
South Wales (touring)
Worcester Cathedral Appeal Auction,
Sotheby's, London
Tribute to Peter Fuller, Beaux Arts Gallery, Bath
Sculptors' Drawings, Cleveland Bridge Gallery,
Bath

1991 *Critics' Choice,* Tribute to Peter Fuller,
Manchester City Art Gallery
Sculpture at Salisbury Cathedral, Chichester
Festival
Summer Exhibition, Beaux Arts Gallery, Bath

PUBLIC COLLECTIONS

Wolverhampton Education Committee
Newport Education Committee
British School in Rome
Welsh Arts Council
Leeds City Council
The Arts Council of Great Britain
Bradford City Art Gallery
Yorkshire Arts Association
Southern Arts Association
Hull City Art Gallery
The Victoria and Albert Museum, London
Peterborough Development Corporation
Milton Keynes Development Corporation
London Borough of Hounslow
Welsh Sculpture Trust
Milton Keynes General Hospital
Hove Museum and Art Gallery, Sussex
Museum of the Human Hand, Lausanne, Switzerland
Hemel Hempstead Arts Trust
Northern Arts Association
Grisedale Theatre in the Forest Trust, Cumbria
Hakone Open Air Museum, Japan
Middlesbrough Borough Council
Haroldwood Hospital, Essex
Bottisham Village College, Cambridge
Tate Gallery, London
The Henry Moore Centre for Sculpture, Leeds
T.S.B. Group plc, London
Hampshire Sculpture Trust

Modern British Masters Volume VI
Published 1992 by Bernard Jacobson Ltd
1992 © Bernard Jacobson Ltd
Typeset by Tiger Typeset
Printed by The Pale Green Press, London

Introduction Photograph by Graham Young, London

June 1992

ISBN 1 872784 09 7

BERNARD JACOBSON GALLERY

14A CLIFFORD STREET   LONDON W1X 1RF

TELEPHONE: 071- 495 8575   FACSIMILE: 071-495 6210